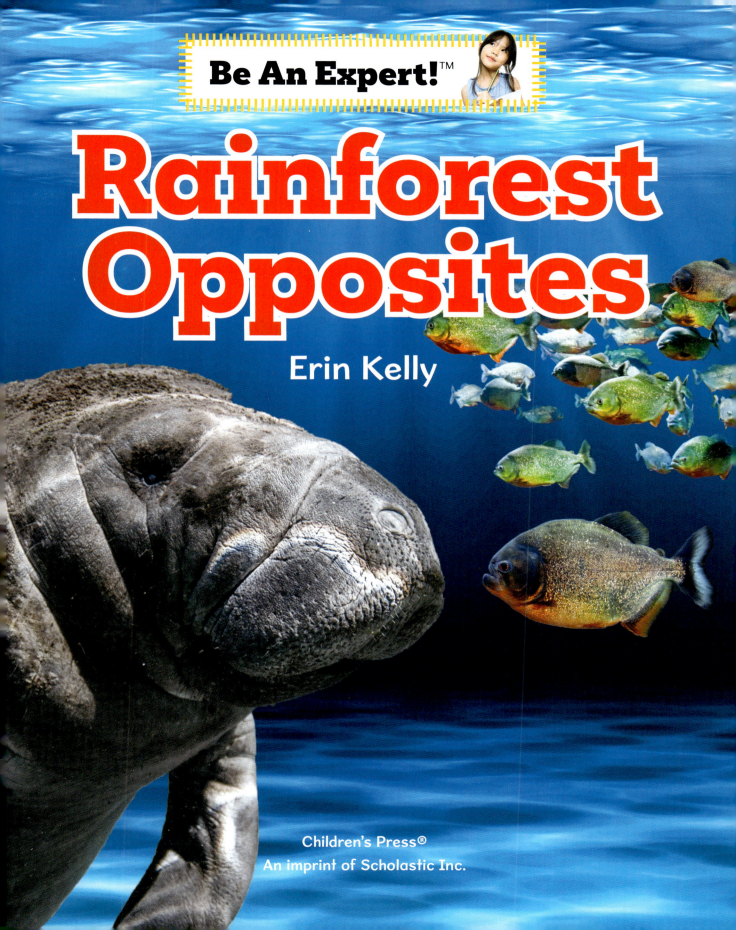

Contents

Big and Small 4

Fast and Slow 6

Know the Names

Be an expert! Get to know the names of these opposites.

Hard and Soft 12

Noisy and Quiet 18

Up and Down 8

Long and Short 10

Open and Closed ... 14

Few and Many 16

All the Opposites 20

Expert Quiz 21

Expert Gear 22

Glossary 23

Index 24

3

Big and Small

The mother gorilla is big.
The baby gorilla is small.

Zoom In

Find more opposites in the big picture.

awake   asleep

dark green   light green

Fast and Slow

The harpy eagle is fast. The sloth is slow.

harpy eagle

Expert Fact

The harpy can fly at 50 miles (80 kilometers) per hour. That's almost as fast as a car drives on the highway. The sloth is the world's slowest **mammal**. It moves slower than one mile per hour.

6

sloth

Up and Down

Some birds stay up in trees. Other birds stay down on the ground.

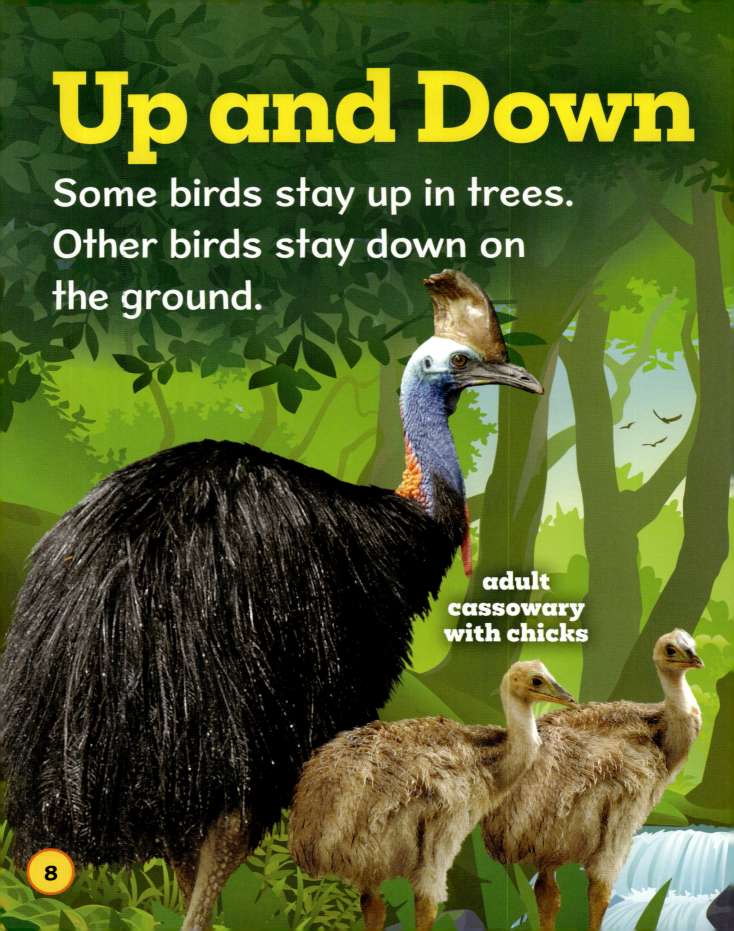

adult cassowary with chicks

Wilson's bird of paradise

Raggiana bird of paradise

Zoom In

Find more opposites in the big picture.

plain | fancy

heavy | light

Long and Short

The toucan has a long **bill**.
The macaw has a short bill.

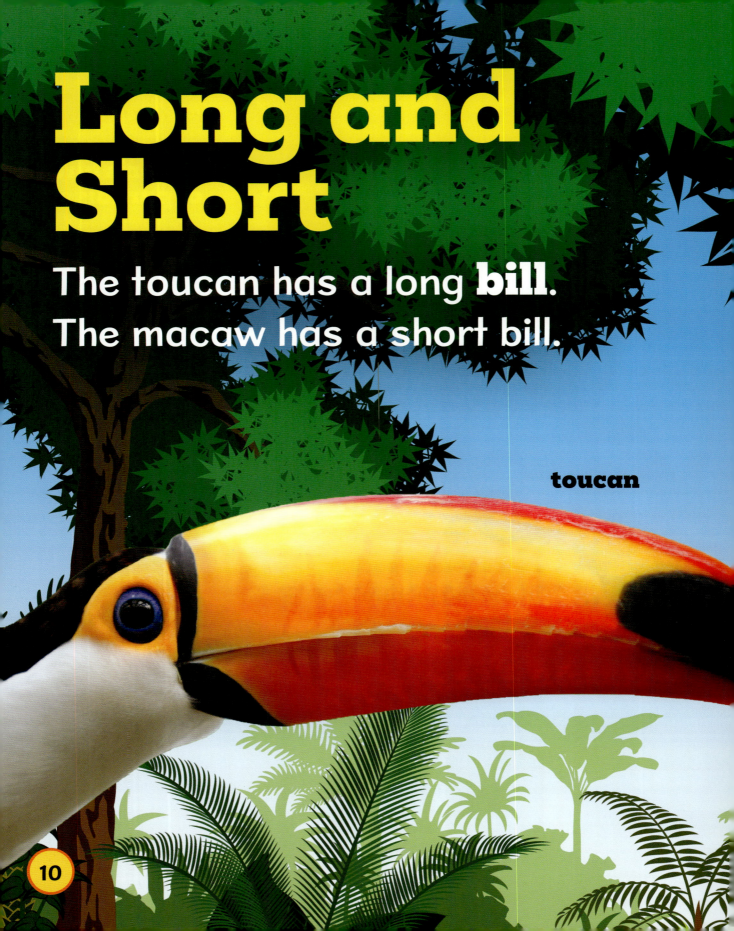

toucan

Animal Answers

Q: Why does a toucan have such a long bill?

A: The toucan uses its bill to pick fruit. The bird can reach fruit on branches that are not strong enough to support its weight.

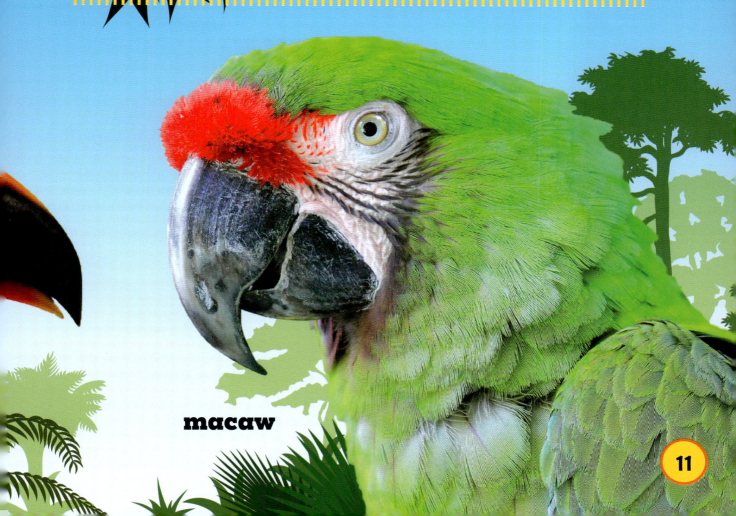

macaw

Hard and Soft

The turtle's shell is hard.
The jaguar's fur is soft.

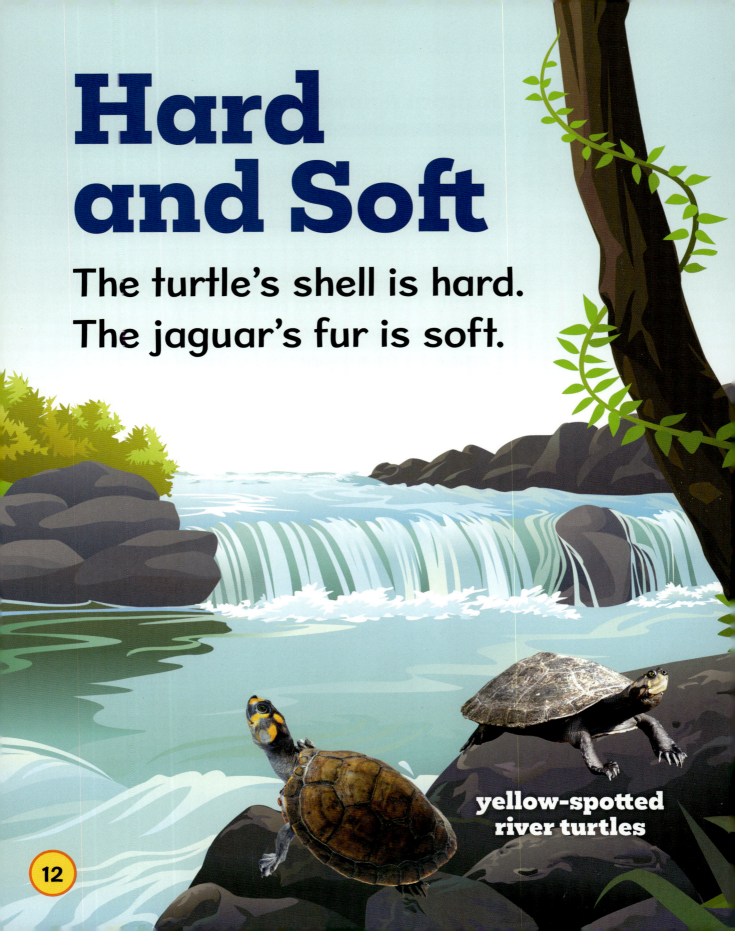

yellow-spotted river turtles

jaguar

Zoom In

Find more opposites in the big picture.

near   far

wet   dry

13

Open and Closed

The caiman's mouth is open.
The giant otter's mouth is closed.

caiman

14

Animal Answers

Q: Why does a caiman rest with its mouth open?

A: A caiman's body gets hot in the rainforest. It opens its mouth so heat can escape. Aah!

giant otter

Few and Many

There are few manatees.
There are many piranhas.

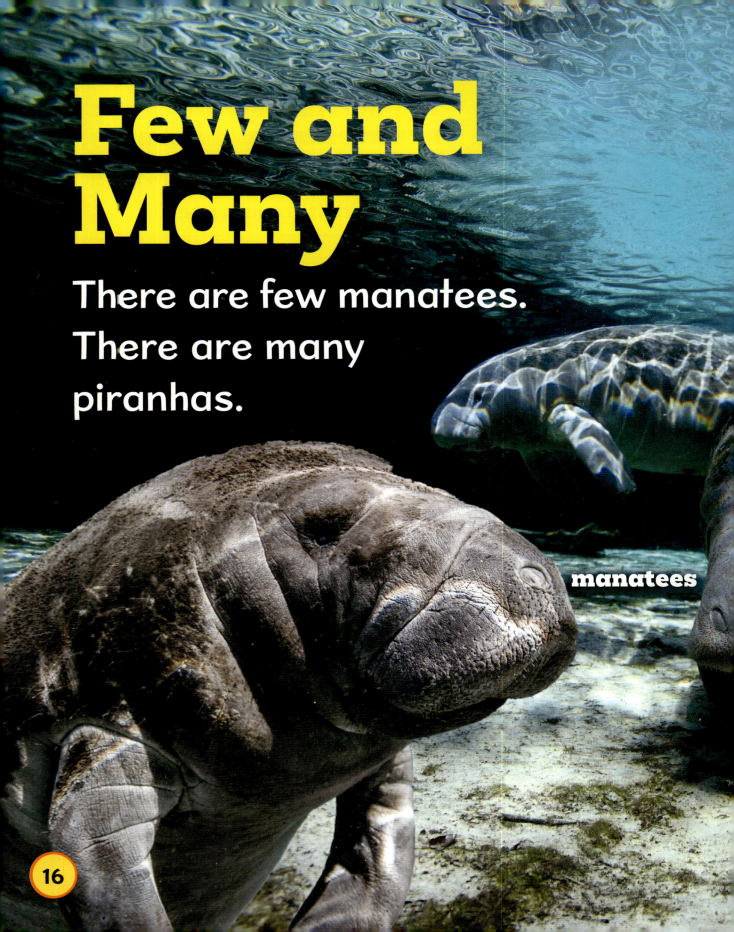

manatees

piranhas

Expert Fact

Piranhas swim in large groups for safety. **Predators** have a hard time picking one fish out of the group.

Noisy and Quiet

The howler monkey is noisy.
The rainbow boa is quiet.

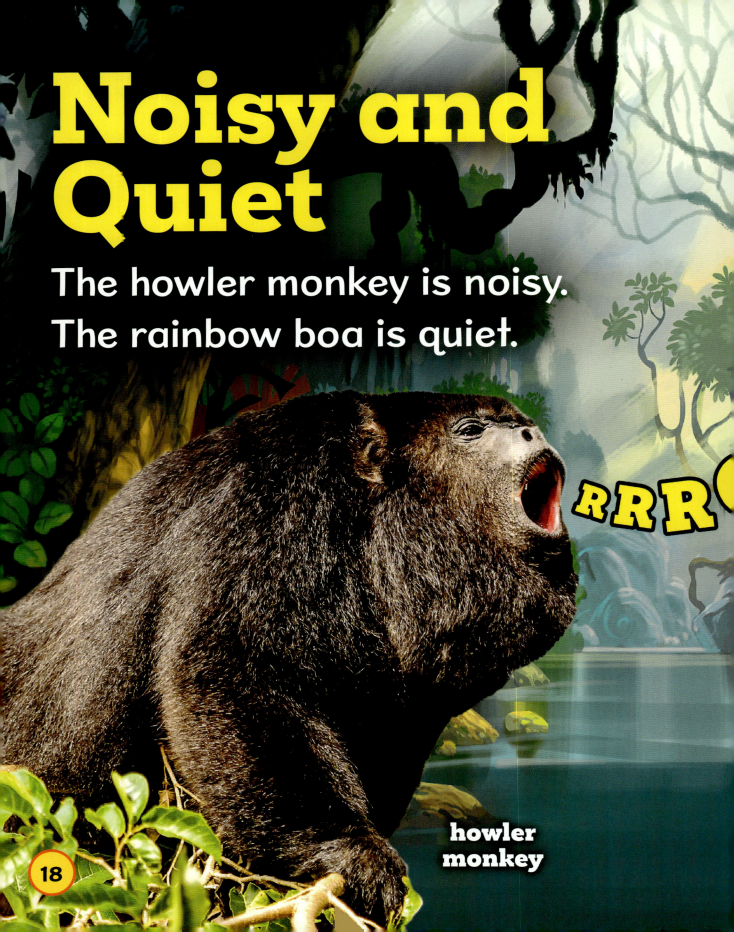

howler monkey

rainbow boa

Expert Fact

The howler monkey is one of the loudest animals in the world. You can hear it from 3 miles (5 kilometers) away!

All the Opposites

There is so much to see in the rainforest. Opposites are fun!

soft

1.

many

2.

slow

5.

long

6.

Expert Quiz

Can you name the opposite of each photo shown here? Then you are an expert! See if someone else can name them too!

3. noisy

4. big

7. up

8. open

Answers: 1. Hard, 2. Few, 3. Quiet, 4. Small, 5. Fast, 6. Short, 7. Down, 8. Closed.

Expert Gear

Meet a rainforest researcher. What gear does she need to study the rainforest **canopy**?

She needs a **helmet**.

She needs **ropes**.

She needs a **notebook**.

She needs a **harness**.

Glossary

bill (BIL): the beak or jaws of a bird.

canopy (KAN-uh-pee): an upper layer of a rainforest.

mammal (MAM-uhl): an animal that has hair and usually gives birth to live babies.

predators (PRED-uh-turz): animals that live by hunting other animals for food.

Index

awake and asleep...4–5

big and small 4–5

bill 10, 11, 23

caiman 14–15

canopy 22, 23

cassowary 8

fast and slow.......... 6–7

few and many...... 16–17

giant otter...............14–15

gorilla 4–5

hard and soft.......12–13

harpy eagle 6–7

heavy and light.......8–9

high and low............ 4–5

howler monkey....18–19

jaguar.................... 12–13

long and short......10–11

macaw 10–11

mammal.................6, 23

manatees.............. 16–17

near and far.........12–13

noisy and quiet ...18–19

open and closed ...14–15

piranhas 16–17

plain and fancy 8–9

Raggiana bird of paradise 9

rainbow boa.........18–19

sloth.......................... 6–7

toucan.................... 10–11

up and down..........8–9

wet and dry 12–13

Wilson's bird of paradise 9

yellow-spotted river turtles..................... 12–13

Library of Congress Cataloging-in-Publication Data
Names: Kelly, Erin Suzanne, 1965– author.
Title: Rain forest opposites/by Erin Kelly.
Other titles: Be an expert! (Scholastic Inc.)
Description: Book edition. | New York: Children's Press, an imprint of Scholastic Inc., 2022. | Series: Be an expert | Includes index. | Audience: Ages 3–5. | Audience: Grades K–1. | Summary: "Big and little. Fast and slow. Open and closed. How many opposites do you know? With this book, you can become an expert! Feel like a pro with exciting photos, expert facts, and fun challenges. Can you name the opposite of quiet or the opposite of down? Try it! Then see if you can pass the Expert Quiz!"—Provided by publisher.
Identifiers: LCCN 2021025671 (print) | LCCN 2021025672 (ebook) | ISBN 9781338797985 (library binding) | ISBN 9781338797992 (paperback) | ISBN 9781338798012 (ebk)
Subjects: LCSH: Rain forest animals—Juvenile literature. | Rain forests—Juvenile literature. | Polarity—Juvenile literature.
Classification: LCC QL112 .K458 2022 (print) | LCC QL112 (ebook) | DDC 591.734—dc23
LC record available at https://lccn.loc.gov/2021025671
LC ebook record available at https://lccn.loc.gov/2021025672

Copyright © 2022 by Scholastic Inc.

All rights reserved. Published by Children's Press, an imprint of Scholastic Inc., *Publishers since 1920*. SCHOLASTIC, CHILDREN'S PRESS, BE AN EXPERT!™, and associated logos are trademarks and/or registered trademarks of Scholastic Inc.

The publisher does not have any control over and does not assume any responsibility for author or third-party websites or their content.

No part of this publication may be reproduced, stored in a retrieval system, or transmitted in any form or by any means, electronic, mechanical, photocopying, recording, or otherwise, without written permission of the publisher. For information regarding permission, write to Scholastic Inc., Attention: Permissions Department, 557 Broadway, New York, NY 10012.

10 9 8 7 6 5 4 3 2 1   22 23 24 25 26

Printed in Heshan, China 62
First edition, 2022

Series produced by Spooky Cheetah Press
Design by The Design Lab, Kathleen Petelinsek

Photos ©: 2 top left gorilla: Mike Walker/Alamy Images; 2 top right eagle: Nick Garbutt/Minden Pictures; 2 center right turtle looking up: Jorge Garcia/VWPics/Alamy Images; 2 center right turtle on rock: Guenter Fischer/Getty Images; 2 bottom right boa: Cynoclub/Dreamstime; 3 top left Lesser bird: Raju Ahmed/Alamy Images; 3 top left cassowary: Dave Watts/Getty Images; 3 top left Wilson's bird: Dubi Shapiro/AGAMI Photo Agency/Alamy Images; 4 bottom: Mike Walker/Alamy Images; 6 center: Nick Garbutt/Minden Pictures; 8 foreground: Dave Watts/Getty Images; 9 top right: Dubi Shapiro/AGAMI Photo Agency/Alamy Images; 9 center: Raju Ahmed/Alamy Images; 12 left: Jorge Garcia/VWPics/Alamy Images; 12 right: Guenter Fischer/Getty Images; 19 top: Cynoclub/Dreamstime; 20 bottom left: Jenhuang99/Dreamstime; 21 center right: Mike Walker/Alamy Images; 21 bottom left: Dubi Shapiro/AGAMI Photo Agency/Alamy Images; 22 main: Courtesy of the TREE Foundation; 23 center bottom: Jenhuang99/Dreamstime.

All other photos © Shutterstock.